The Art of Manipulation

10 Powerful Techniques to Effectively Deal with Others, Influence Human Behavior, and Finally Get the Results You Want

Nick Anderson

Table of Contents

Introduction

A good friend of mine, Brian, can sell anything. By anything, I mean everything.

I am fully convinced, to this very day, that Brian can sell used toilet paper. That's how persuasive he is.

Forget about selling ice to Eskimos. Brian can sell used toilet paper. In fact, I have seen with my own two eyes Brian convincing a sales prospect who already rejected the offer several times to buy a much bigger deal.

I wish I could tell you that sales ability is inborn. It would be great if that was the case because sales people all over the United States and elsewhere could have a ready excuse. How easy would it be to say, "I wasn't born this way?"

Well, it turns out that Brian wasn't born like that. Far from it. In fact, when I first met him, he didn't have much confidence in his ability to persuade people.

What happened? What changed?

Well, this book is a discussion of the many lessons I learned from master persuaders, negotiators, and yes, manipulators.

My friend Brian is just the tip of the iceberg. I've talked to lawyers, negotiators, all sorts of sales people, executives, sales managers, call center operatives, and all sorts of specialists. These people live or die based on their ability to persuade others to their point of view.

It would be great if all they needed to do was to gently push people from somewhat being undecided about their offer to a full-on yes. What makes a lot of these people different is that they can persuade somebody who has said no.

I'm not talking about just a firm, direct to the point no. I'm talking about violent opposition.

I can't even begin to tell you how many times my mind has been blown by seeing these people just work their magic. What's going on?

Well, the more I researched the art of manipulation, the more I realized that it is really just the art of human communication and persuasion... but on steroids.

This book will help you become a better manipulator.

For you to fully appreciate the value of this book, I want you to lose all the negative connections of that word. I'm sure, since childhood, you, like everybody else, have been told that being manipulative or manipulating people is a bad thing.

The truth is, there is really a thin line separating effective communication and persuasion, and manipulation and exploitation or abuse. A lot of it turns on your intent. A lot of it also turns on the proficiency of the person you're dealing with.

To say that there is this bright line between persuasion and manipulation, and that manipulation is one and the same as exploitation, misses the point.

You have to understand that when you are facing a stone wall of rejection, you have to dig deep into your persuasion toolbox to get the job done. The art of manipulation really is all about just sending the right signals and working with the hand that's dealt to you in light of human psychology.

It is not black magic. It doesn't involve twisting somebody's arm. It definitely doesn't require or need any force. You just have to rely on the force of your personality.

You have to believe that you can do it. You have to be convinced that you have it in you to manipulate your situation and your communication skills to get the results you want.

Who Wants to Manipulate Others Anyway?

We have been programmed for so long to think that manipulation is a bad thing. We lose sight of the fact that any kind of success requires persuasion.

I wish I could tell you that you only need to state your case clearly and get people to understand how they would benefit. But it isn't that simple.

If you've ever been involved in any kind of negotiation, you can bet that a lot of the people that you are facing are sharks. They know that this is a good deal, but they want more, and more, and more. They also want to position you in such a way that you might not get the optimal end of the bargain.

The art of manipulation is both defensive and proactive. By learning how to manipulate people's perception of the value proposition you bring to the table, you put yourself at a competitive advantage. You also end up defending yourself from exploitation.

Remember, there's a big difference between manipulating and out and out exploitation and abuse. A lot of it has to do with your intent.

If your intention is just to make sure that you get what's coming to you fair and square, you need to master the art of manipulation. If your intent, on the other hand, is to get something that you're not entitled to and you want to pull one over other people, then you are walking on thin ice.

You have to understand that the better you get at manipulation, the easier it would be for you to step over the line and become an abusive person. Once you develop that reputation, it's going to be very hard to put that toothpaste back in the tube. It's just not going to happen as quickly and as painlessly as you think.

It's a really good idea to draw a limit or a boundary between the manipulation skills that you're learning and flat out exploitation.

What is Manipulation Anyway?

Manipulation is all about motivating other people to do what you want them to do.

Everybody's got their interests. Everybody thinks they know that they have their best interest in mind. Unfortunately, there are many situations where people are not all that efficient.

They basically look at the deal in front of them in a very narrow way. It often takes manipulation to get people to look at the bigger picture.

I remember being part of a sales team where we approached a vice president of a distribution company. The guy didn't even want to give us the time of day because he was just so focused on the fact that our company already had a deal with his firm.

Why do we want to rock the boat? Why should we look into other product lines? Why should we tap into other parts of their network? He was only looking at the deal from his perspective, which involves a pretty attractive monthly revenue stream.

Instead of focusing on what we wanted and presenting our position that way, we made a big deal out of the statement the CEO of his company made.

His firm's CEO gave a public statement during an investor conference call saying that they wanted to expand their national reach and diversify the revenue streams.

Once we zeroed in on that and tied that into the opportunity that we bring to the table, the vice president's eyes lit up. And when we started breaking down the numbers, it's as if he wanted to grab the pen from my hand so he can sign the contract before me.

The art of manipulation often boils down to letting others realize the opportunity they've been blind to. It can also mean letting them get a full picture of the value they can produce if they partner with other people.

The big problem with manipulation and persuasion to a big degree is that we tend to get tunnel vision. I'm sure I'm not saying anything controversial or anything particularly new if I tell you that human beings are selfish. We're all out for number one.

When we focus so much on ourselves, it's very easy to lose sight of other people's needs and our connection to other people. These are lost opportunities because it is precisely these connections that can take our income, career, company results, and yes, personal happiness, to the next level.

When you learn how to manipulate interpersonal signals and situations, you're not just pushing your own agenda. You're also putting yourself in a position to help other people. You are unlocking value.

If that is your mindset, you will go far with these techniques. On the other hand, if your mindset is to get an unfair advantage, pull one over them, or trick or deceive people, chances are, you're not really manipulating. Instead, you are deceiving, defrauding, lying, cheating.

You have to understand that there is a big difference between those abusive and exploitative behaviors and manipulation.

When you manipulate, you're not just using words. You are also employing nonverbal signals, body language, as well as the tone of your voice and your facial gestures. You're also lining up your message and the emotional signals that you're sending out with the situation surrounding your conversation.

When you sit down and try to practice the art of manipulation in a clear, concise and precise way, you are basically acting like a maestro in a philharmonic concert. You move your baton around as these different signals come from your end and from the person that you are talking to.

It's all about aligning these signals, some you can control, most you can't, to get to the result you want.

This book will offer you 10 effective manipulation techniques that will help you get the better deal and potentially provide better value.

Chapter 1 : Use Scare To Relief Technique To Trigger Quick Results

Have you ever had a dream that is so scary that you are just scared out of your wits? You imagine yourself somewhere and you're just thinking to yourself, "I hope this is the worst of it."

Maybe you were shocked in the dream. Maybe something really bad happened to you. Perhaps you were going through a tremendous amount of pain. Just when you thought that things can't get any worse, they do.

What was going through your mind when you wake up, maybe in a cold sweat, and you realize that it was all a dream? I can bet that you felt that huge surge of relief.

You probably felt really good. After all, who wants to get murdered, crushed, get one's heart broken, or any other disasters that we normally encounter in our nightmares?

This experience is very easy to remember because of the stark contrast between the fear that you were going through, and the sense of relief that you got when you realized that your dream wasn't real. That sense of relief feels good.

In fact, when we feel any kind of pressure or discomfort, we yearn for that moment of relief. This takes place subconsciously.

So when you set up situations during negotiations that trigger this contrast between fear and relief, you gain a tremendous bargaining advantage. You can bet that people would want to gain that sense of relief after you have painted the worst case scenario.

How does this work in a sales setting? Well, first, you have to lay out what could go wrong.

Now, we all know that, at this very moment, as you read this book, a plane could fall out of the sky and burn down the cafe that you are relaxing in. We also know that the chances of that event happening are quite rare.

Expert negotiators who use the fear and relief contrast method use likely threats. These must be scary situations that are probable.

The problem with automatically jumping to the worst case scenario is, for the most part, the worst situations never come to pass. They are too improbable. Too many things have to line up for them to happen. While they are very scary, people also know that they have a higher chance of being hit by lightning twice than those improbable events happening.

If you want to get people to see your side and agree with you during negotiations, you can use this fear and relief contrast by talking about fears that they already have now.

For example, if you are negotiating a large marketing contract with a traditional manufacturing company that already makes millions of dollars a year, you're not going to start out by saying, "Your company's going to shut down because people wouldn't care about your brand. There's just too much competition out there."

They know that that's the worst case scenario. But they also know that that is not immediate enough. Just like any other company, they have contingency plans. They also have many different product lines. That isn't very likely.

You can, however, point out the fact that they use traditional media. They send out press releases, they advertise on TV and radio, and they even take out newspaper ads. When you paint a nightmare scenario of social media search engine results and mobile advertising enabling their upstart competitors to become more visible, you will get their attention.

How come? They're already aware of this. They may be confused about it, they might not see the big picture or they might not be aware of the full implications and consequences of these trends, but they are aware of them. That's when you trigger the fear.

And you build it up by mentioning statistics involving the rise of social media advertising, the rise of mobile devices used, and the fact that by a certain year, almost all people will be using mobile devices to access the internet. In other words, their legacy marketing system will be obsolete. This creates the fear.

And then you follow it up with the message of relief. You say that, "If you start with our firm now, we can ensure that your brand continues to be relevant. Your company will continue to grow and reach whoever you need to reach, regardless of the devices they use and regardless of the change in consumer tastes and communication preferences."

See the contrast? Focus on something that is probable and something that the person you're negotiating with is already aware of it. Fully flesh it out. Spell out the implication for them.

Ideally, you should also mention case studies. These are companies that ignored the rise of social media and got punished for it. Maybe they are now a boutique brand or, worse yet, they've gone belly up.

It's all about setting a contrast between a sense of helplessness, hopelessness and fear, and the solution that you bring. Your solution is what brings relief. And guess what? People become very open-minded at that point.

In a study conducted at the University of Opole in Poland by the University's social sciences and humanities department, researchers Richard Nawrat and Dariuz Dolinski conducted five experiments where they tested the ability of fear, followed by relief. They tested whether inducing fear followed quickly by relief can get people to comply with certain instructions.

These experiments involved people crossing the road in the wrong spot. Another involved people who parked their cars where they shouldn't, and another involved breaking traffic regulations. The other two experiments involved making changes in the conditions of the previous two.

It turns out that if you were just going to scare people into complying, it is not going to change their behavior all that much. In the first experiment involving people jaywalking, hearing a policeman blowing a whistle was not enough to get people to change their behavior.

On the other hand, people who felt a tremendous amount of anxiety when they saw a note that they thought was a ticket on their windshield wiper or on their door were more likely to be more compliant.

It's easy to see why. They felt threatened because they thought it was an actual ticket. But when they were relieved that it was just a warning, they were more likely to change their behavior.

Simply scaring people doesn't work. **There has to be an increase in anxiety or fear, followed by a deep sense of relief**, like finding out you didn't get a ticket. You start viewing that situation as a close call and you're more likely to change your behavior.

Now let's look at the next manipulation technique.

Chapter 2: "That's Not All" – Best Ways (and Timings) to Sweeten Your Offer

If you're trying to sell something or get people to sign on the dotted line, one of the most difficult situations to find yourself in involves a prospect who is almost there.

You did your sales presentation. You communicated your message very clearly. It seems they have a good understanding of the value the deal has to offer them. It's as if they're sending the right signals to you, but they're not quite there.

One of the most powerful ways to manipulate people to get off the fence is the "that's not all" technique. This negotiation tactic revolves around the perceived completion of the deal. When you are presenting your offer, you probably outlined the major points of the deal.

One of the drawbacks of showing your hand completely is that you paint yourself in a corner. What if it turns out that your prospect needs a little extra push for them to sign at the dotted line? By that point, you really have no bullets left because you have put all the goodies in your offer on the table.

Everything is transparent. Each party knows what they are getting. Everything is on the line. There's nothing left.

The "that's not all" technique is a very powerful manipulative tool because it exploits the human tendency to want a better deal. It may not be that big of an improvement but if we get the impression that we are getting something extra, we are more likely to make a decision.

Take the case of Bob and Nancy. Bob was trying to get Nancy to buy a set of collectibles. Bob laid out all the items that are going to be in the set. He knew full well that Nancy wanted all the items in the set.

In fact, Nancy did not hide her emotions and reactions during the presentation. She was oohing and aahing throughout the whole presentation. She wasn't shy about it. You can read her like a book. Bob thought he had Nancy in the palm of his hands. He thought this was a slam dunk.

However, when it came time to get Nancy to sign on the dotted line, she balked. This was pretty stressful for Bob. He did not hide the price. From the get-go, he said this is how much the set of collectibles would cost. Neither did he leave anything out when it comes to what is involved in the deal. He said that all these items are going to be part of the deal. He produced a list. Nancy went through the list. Everybody was on the same page.

What went wrong? The problem was Bob painted himself in a corner. He did not leave out that extra push that could get Nancy to seal the deal.

A master manipulator would play the game this way:

Scenario #1

Instead of listing out all items in the collectible series, leave one item out that adds a tremendous amount of value to the series. It is not the main part of the series but it definitely completes the series. Its value is obvious and serious collectors would want to have that item as part of any series.

However, judging by previous sales of the same collectible series, it's okay to leave that item out. In this scenario, you make the offer to Nancy to sign on the dotted line. She hesitates and then you present the missing item from the list, but instead of saying that this item completes the series, you present it as an add-on.

That's right. You position it as a premium that she shouldn't be getting but as part of this special deal, she gets it if she pays this for the same price as the rest of the package. You get her to try to sign the purchase invoice, but right before you say, "Wait a minute. That's not all. Here's an extra item," and usually this is enough to push people over the line.

In a 1986 study conducted at Santa Clara University, a research group headed by Jerry Burger used the "that's not all" technique using additional packages of cookies after prospects indicated they were thinking of buying something else.

When you have a prospect who is obvious about buying a package but is kind of on the fence, use the "that's not all" technique involving an extra item to get them to make up their mind. This extra push has been shown to increase sales by 70%.

Scenario #2

When Nancy looks over the final offer and checks out the package price, you give her a few seconds to think about the deal and then when it becomes obvious that she's going to hesitate, tell her, "That's not all. If you sign up now, we're going to give you reduction."

Now the reduction can be 10% or 20%. It totally depends on your perception of her willingness to buy. If she appears to be very eager to buy but is just slightly hesitating, a lower discount would work. Ten percent should be able to do to the trick. However, if it's obvious that she still has a somewhat significant reservation but is almost there, you might want to offer the twenty percent.

In the same Santa Clara University experiment, sixty students were approached at bake sale kiosks put up around the college campus. When students were not given a choice as to the price of a baked good, they were not more likely to buy items than students who were given a discount. If they feel that they can negotiate, they are more likely to buy.

When you give the price to Nancy and then follow up with an offer of a lower price, she is given a chance to negotiate. This increases, according to the Santa Clara study, the probability of a sale by up to 85%.

Mechanics of the "That's Not All" Technique

To maximize the effectiveness of this technique, it's important to give the prospect enough time to consider the deal. You shouldn't just give your price and then quickly follow it up with a lower price.

You have to remember the effectiveness of this manipulation tactic revolves around the perception of negotiation. The prospect must believe that they are in control of the process or are getting something that they are otherwise not going to get. This is the key factor in the effectiveness of the "that's not all" technique.

If at the back of their head they already knew that there is a missing piece in the package, it's probably going to be very hard for you to convince your prospect to buy at the original price or even at the negotiated price. They already know that you have something up your sleeve.

They want to feel that they are getting something from you that you normally would not give. This is why it's crucial to present the extra item on the discount as some sort of sacrifice or some sort of special deal.

It is no surprise that one of the stock lines used by experienced salespeople goes along the lines of "Normally, I don't cut this deal but since you're so special, let me do it for you." Of course, salespeople throughout the years have come up with their own variation of that line. Still, certain basic elements have to be in your "that's not all" presentation.

First, you have to make the prospect feel special. You cannot give them the impression that you always cut deals like this with everybody you come across.

For example, if you're trying to get them to buy a package at the original price of a hundred dollars, don't let them know that you normally let that package go for $60. Tell them, "Normally, the price of this is set at a $100, but since you are a special person and I know that you need this and we're really trying to bend over backwards and make our customers happy, I will give it to you for $80."

Make it look like a sacrifice. If they know that you routinely give out the same or better deals, then they are more likely to balk.

Another key factor here is scarcity. Let them know that this is a one-time thing or that there is some sort of time pressure. The "that's not all" technique works best with a sense of urgency. Nothing creates that sense of urgency better than the impression that you're going to run out of stock.

You can also create the impression that the program is about to run out. Furthermore, if you are holding a liquidation or you're going out of business, this helps pump up the buyer's sense of urgency.

Ultimately, this is a very powerful manipulative technique because it draws its effectiveness from an imbalance of information. If you're selling a product for $100 knowing full well that you buy it from the factory at $20, then you have a lot of room to move. You can play that "that's not all game" all day every day.

The moment your prospect knows that you get this stuff for $20, then all bets are off. You're going to have a tough time convincing that person. You better come up with a better product positioning or after-sales service or any sort of justification to close the deal. After all, they already know the value of the product that they're getting.

The second key aspect of this technique involves tuning into the prospect's need to feel like they got the better end of the negotiation. We all like to feel like we're heroes. So, in this scenario, you feel like a hero if you paid $70 for something that the salesperson is trying to unload for $100.

In your mind, you save $30; you're a hero. Little do you know that store actually gets its stock for $20. They still make a profit at $20.

Exploit that need to be a hero. Everybody has that. Everybody likes to feel that they matter. Everybody likes to feel that they are competent. Everybody likes to feel that they are intelligent.

So, when you tell the other party that you're putting my back against the wall, but guess what? I give up. I'll drop the price. Let's get this over with. They feel like a hero, and you walk away with something close to what you wanted initially.

In the nutshell, what matters most is that you get the other side do what you wanted, and making them feel like hero is the best way to get them into action.

Whenever you're trying to sell somebody on an option, it's not unusual for people to have different alternatives to choose from. For example, you're trying to get somebody to buy a specific car make and model when at the back of their minds they also want other brands and models. They can't quite make up their mind.

Obviously, they're interested enough in what you have to offer; otherwise, they wouldn't be talking to you in the first place. However, you can sense that they are torn among different choices.

One of the most effective ways to get the prospect to take "simplify" their choice by focusing on your option is to confuse them among the different choices. You then follow up with a simple phrasing of the benefits of your offer.

In a classic study out of the University of Arkansas in 1999, researchers were offered packages of notecards. In one scenario, they would offer it in dollars and in another scenario, they would offer it in pennies. Both are worth the same, but when the package was shown in pennies, the salesperson would say that this is 'a bargain.

It turns out that whenever a prospect is confused and they are given messaging that simplifies the confusion, they are more likely to be persuaded. The study had two scenarios. One involves a salesperson going door-to-door selling an eight-notecard package that had attractive pictures on them. In the control group, the salesperson would tell the prospect that the package costs a total of $3.

In the disruption variation of this experiment, the salesperson would say that these notecards cost 300 pennies. They would wait for a pause and then they would say they would simplify things to the prospect by saying $3. In the next scenario, the salesperson would say that the package costs $3 and then after a moment's pause, they would follow up with a phrase "It's a bargain."

Finally, in the condition being tested by the experiment - disrupt and then reframe condition - the prospect was told that the eight-notecards package costs three hundred pennies. After a moment's pause, the salesperson would say "That is $3; you're getting a bargain!"

The technique is very powerful because when you get the person confused about converting three hundred pennies into $3, you get their trust when you simplify matters for them. You basically say subconsciously that you have their back.

When you convert the confusing detail into something that they can easily understand, they are more favorable to you. They are more likely to trust you because you simplified something that was confusing for them. They didn't have to mentally work as hard. By following up with a suggested reframing of "That's a bargain," you are making a recommendation clear.

It's very easy for them to think that this conclusion came from them. They know that you simplified things for them when you said, "That's $3." What follows is an opinion. You first begin with a fact, which they would agree with. They can easily verify that fact. However, they are very vulnerable to the opinion that you quickly fed them.

Just how effective is this manipulation tactic? Well, according to the Arkansas researchers, this technique accounted for a sales effectiveness of 70%. For people who were being persuaded normally, only 30% of people bought. That's a significant difference. It all boils down to trust.

When you simplify something that is seemingly confusing to somebody, they can't help but feel a sense of relief. They also can't help but feel that you are to be trusted or at least you are a positive person.

Believe it or not this technique works well with online marketing. A lot of affiliate pages available on the Internet take what would otherwise be confusing niche information and simplify key facts that are easily verifiable.

Since most people don't have all the time in the world to research each and every piece of information they come across on the Internet, they come to trust these pages. As they go through the materials, they scan and they quickly check their own personal knowledge about certain facts being mentioned.

If enough of these line up with facts that the prospect knows are real, they are more likely to trust the page. When the articles are recommending a certain option, these readers are more likely to be persuaded.

Your job is to simplify the situation for the prospect and this will immediately build your rapport with your prospect and he will trust your guidance, which makes selling your product, service or any idea.

Chapter 4 : Manipulate in Small Increments

One of the most well-known and widely practiced sales technique is the "foot in the door" technique. You basically make an initial small request that seems innocent enough. It doesn't take much effort on the part of the other party to go along with your request.

Maybe you're asking questions, maybe you're asking for an opinion, maybe you're asking for a small task that they're already doing. Whatever form it takes, it seems like it doesn't really take much time or effort to comply with your request.

What's really happening is that you are manipulating in small increments. You're getting your foot in the door. And, once your foot is in the door, you can crack that door open wider and wider in substantial increments.

The first request is fairly straightforward and easy enough for the other party to comply with. You then let some time pass, and then you get in contact again with the other party and make a larger request. After some time has passed, you then make a very big request.

This works tremendously in sales. One common way this is done is when people are asked online to fill out a survey. They are then asked to check out free products. After that point, they are then offered discounts on related products.

If you're paying attention to this process, one pattern should jump out at you. It is a filtering pattern.

Basically, it boils down to this: not everybody will answer a questionnaire. Only people who are interested in the overall subject or topic of the questionnaire would bother to reply. This is a filtration mechanism.

For example, if I advertise a survey on people looking to apply to graduate school, who do you think will respond? That's right, only people who are thinking of applying to graduate school.

At the back of their minds, they're curious and they've already been doing their research. Some people are more serious than others. Regardless, these are the people that are more likely to take the test.

People who are already in graduate school or people who have other plans wouldn't be interested. They wouldn't bother.

Once the survey is completed, I can then conclude with an email collection form in the form of an online email-based seminar. I would thank the survey participants for filling out the form. I would then also invite them to sign up for this free graduate school seminar.

It's completely free, no obligations, nothing to buy. Basically, they will be receiving information that would fill them in on all parts of the graduate school application process. It doesn't matter what specific program they're applying to. This applies to all schools and organizations.

Chances are, a significant percentage of people who have finished the survey would want to sign up for that online email-based seminar. After all, it's absolutely free.

Do you see what happened here? You basically started out asking for one request, and now you're following up with another request.

Once these people sign up, not all of them would read their emails. This is why it's crucial to get as many people to sign up for that mailing list because there is a conversion funnel you're going through.

If you start out with 100 people, you're lucky if maybe 30 or 10 people would open their emails. In every email you send, you then offer people to join another mailing list where they would get a free report on how to apply to graduate school.

The series that they signed up to is more general. It tells them the whole application process. The new list that you're marketing tries to persuade the recipient to try out secret steps or more efficient ways.

Generally, the best timing for this is near the end of the seminar. At that point, people are already familiar with how to apply and how much of a headache it would be. A lot of them are scared because it seems so complicated and it's bureaucratic. And then all of a sudden, there is this offer making things simple. And it's still free.

So when they sign up, they get another series of freebies that breaks it down. Everything is more efficient, but it still takes work, time, effort and focus.

Near the end of that series, you then go into the hard sell. You sell them a service that makes the whole graduate school application process a breeze. They just need to fill out a form, and regardless of how many programs they're applying to and regardless of how many hurdles they have to clear, the service will take care of them. All of this is provided in one neat little prize package.

This is a classic sales funnel, but it employs the foot in the door technique. Each step of the process has a filtration system, but also has requests. They're invited to join.

Although the numbers quickly get reduced, it wouldn't matter because if you pump enough people in the front end of the funnel, enough will make it through so you can sell quite a large amount of the final product.

This technique was discovered in a famous paper out of Stanford University by the researchers Scott Fraser and Nathan Freedman. In their study, a group of housewives were split up into four study groups.

The researchers called Group 1 via phone and asked them a few questions regarding the household items they were using. After three days, the researchers called the housewives who responded to their questions. They requested that they allow a group of researchers to come over and study the household items being used in their homes.

For study Group 2, the housewives were called. They were told that there was a survey, but they weren't asked to take it. After three days has passed, the researchers called again and they asked these participants if they would allow researchers to come over to observe household items.

In Group 3, the housewives were given information regarding the requesting person. After they became familiar with the person making the request, they were asked if they would allow researchers to come over.

Finally, for Group 4, no introduction was made. These housewives were basically called and asked, "Can we come over to observe you use certain household items?"

Freedman and Fraser's findings were quite surprising. In Group 1, which involved incremental manipulation, 52.8 % of the housewives allowed 5 to 6 strangers to come to their home. In the fourth group, which involved no introduction and went straight to the big request, 22.2% approved of the big request.

This study proves that when you start the manipulation process using a small request that is fairly easy to comply with, you build a rapport with the other party. You start earning their trust. Once the initial contact concludes positively, you can then make a bigger request.

As I have mentioned in the description of online selling above, the "foot in the door" sales technique really boils down to filtration, building trust, and authority.

How can you apply this technique in real life? Well, you can start out by asking your friend to borrow their car to go to the store. They know that your car is in the shop and the store is not all that far, so they let you borrow their car.

Let some time pass, and then ask them if you can borrow their car to visit your aunt in another state. Tell them that it will probably take you about a week. If it's their second car, there's a strong chance that they would let you borrow.

This is quite a big request, but you actually have a high chance of succeeding. First of all, you are their friend. You are not a complete and total stranger. There is some level of familiarity there. Second, you've already established the initial pattern when they let you borrow their car to go to the store.

Another form this takes involves workplace situations. When a boss or supervisor asks an employee to work one hour overtime, it's not unusual for the employee to readily comply if the employer asks for a full day's work over the weekend.

The Secret to the Technique

There are several factors at work here. I've already mentioned the power of familiarity, authority, credibility and trust. But there's also a sense of obligation.

Once we allow ourselves to trust at a certain level and it seems that nothing really bad happened or nothing disruptive happened, we're actually quite likely to repeat that pattern, but on a larger scale. This involves bonding. This involves deeper levels of trust and familiarity.

Chapter 5 : Use Apparent Initial Failure To Get What You (Really) Want

The "foot in the door" manipulation technique is all about starting with small, easy-to-comply-with requests. In fact, they seem so innocuous.

People would ask you, "Hi. Could you take a survey?" or "Would you like this small sample?" It doesn't take much, so you go along. And then they ask for more and more and more. You start small, and then you scale up.

Believe it or not, the precise opposite of that process also works. This is the "door in the face" manipulation technique. You ask for something really big from the get go.

Basically, at the beginning, there's almost no intro. You just basically lay it into the person you're requesting from.

How many times have you talked to your buddy and asked for 500 bucks? Chances are, they probably would come up with all sorts of reasons not to lend to you.

One common answer would be, "Hey, I would have given it to you. I'm sorry, but I just paid the rent" or "Why did you just call me now? I just spent that much money on the big screen TV. I would have lent it to you if you just called an hour earlier." You know the drill.

Believe it or not, when you ask a big request at first that is almost guaranteed to be turned down, you can actually set up the other party to comply with a smaller request.

What happens when you started out with $500, and then after you get the explanation, you change things up and you say, "Okay, can you lend me 50 bucks?" Chances are quite good that your friend or relative will fork over the cash.

What happened? Well, first of all, you have successfully manipulated their sense of relief. You have set it up so that $500 is simply too much. Their alarm bells go off and they get all panicky. But once you tone it down to the actual amount that you wanted, which is $50 in the first place, they're more likely to comply.

This is a very effective technique because you are manipulating two key areas of human psychology. First is the sense of relief. When people enter a state of relief, they are more likely to be persuaded. They are more likely to go along.

Second, you trigger the mindset that they put one over you. You know full well that your friend who said that he just paid the rent really didn't just pay the rent. He just doesn't want to lend you money. The same goes with the buddy who said that they just bought a big screen TV.

But when you say, "Can I borrow $50 instead?" or "Can you give me whatever little amount you can spare?" they feel that they put one over you. This is a very powerful feeling, so they are more likely to comply with your request.

It's like they're throwing chump change. They think that they won, when in reality, all you wanted was that 50 bucks or spare change.

The Keys to Success with "Door in the Face"

The key to this technique is to come off as unreasonable. You have to present your initial offer in such an extravagant way.

When you say, "Can you let me borrow $5,000 or $500," it's big. It comes out of nowhere.

You have to make sure that the request will be turned down. This is important. Because if the request seems reasonable enough, although substantial, then you're not going to trigger the sense of relief or the sense of victory or satisfaction on the part of the person you're trying to persuade. Size, in this situation, matters.

This technique was discovered by researcher Robert Cialdini in 1975. Also known as **"Rejection then Retreat"** negotiation tactic, "the door in the face" technique was tested out on three groups of experiment participants.

The first group of people were asked if they would volunteer as counselors to a group of kids with behavioral problems and a delinquency track record two hours every week over two years. When this group turned down the request, the researchers asked them a second time, but this time they were asked to take the juvenile delinquents to the zoo for a single day.

Group 2 was only asked if they would take the juvenile delinquents to the zoo.

Group 3 was told about the two-year counseling program that they could select, but they were only asked if they would like to take the juvenile delinquents to the zoo.

Among the three groups, Group 1 had the highest rate of compliance. Group 2 had the lowest rate of compliance. This shows that when you start with an unreasonable request, you can condition the prospect to a more reasonable and easier to manage request later on.

Based on the 50% success rate, Cialdini's experiment yielded the "door in the face" technique can be a very powerful manipulation tool.

For example, if you wanted your very busy sister to watch your kid for a few hours while you go to a seminar, one of the best ways to do this is to ask her initially to babysit for a full day. Given how busy your sister is, that's a guaranteed rejection.

You then quickly follow up and say, "What if you just watch my son for a couple of hours while I go to the seminar?" You are more likely to get a positive response.

Success Factors

As I've mentioned earlier, you trigger a sense of relief when you scale down your response to the request you originally wanted to make in the first place. You also trigger a sense that the person doing you the favor is winning in the negotiations.

It's important to note that for this technique to succeed, you have to observe two rules. First, the exact same person must make both requests. You can't ask your sister to watch your kid, and then the next day your husband makes the request. That won't work.

This technique depends on social bonds and social connection. The person you're requesting from must be made to feel that they're doing you a favor. It has to be personal.

The second factor is that you have to quickly follow up the initial failed request. So make it look like you have scaled down the request. You're basically giving up on your original request and stepping down to something that is more reasonable to them.

This sense of immediacy is crucial because the sense of relief that they get won't be there if you let enough time pass. If you make a request and then you wait a couple of months for a smaller request, chances are, your small requests are not going to go anywhere.

You have to follow up quickly. Manipulate and exploit that sense of relief that they're feeling.

Chapter 6: Lure People In Using a Lowball Offer

You'd be surprised as to how stubborn people can get once they have mentally bought into anything. This applies across the board. It doesn't matter the setting.

Once you convince people that your offer is a good deal, a lot of times, it's going to be very hard for them to back off their initial agreement to that deal. That's right, even if you raise the price or you change the conditions later on, it's surprising to see how many people would stick to their original decision.

This actually happens quite a bit online. Have you ever gone comparison shopping for products? Have you ever come across a website that offers ridiculously low prices for all the products you're looking for?

Did you get all excited? Did you fill up your shopping cart by clicking on item after item? Did you get all pumped up by the tremendous amount of money that you're saving? Maybe you were saving hundreds of dollars, or maybe even thousands.

Wasn't it such a letdown when you click the checkout button and it turns out that you have to pay extra for shipping and handling?

Many people fall for this tried and proven technique. Welcome to the world of the lowball manipulation strategy. It all boils down to getting people to emotionally buy in because of a deal that's very good.

I'm not talking about too good to be true. I'm talking about a very good deal. This still has to be in the realm of possibility and practicality. I'm not talking about scams here.

It turns out that the deal that you thought you had was no deal because of changed conditions. In the case of low cost comparison sites, the changed condition, of course, is the shipping and handling fee.

A lot of those sites actually charge the same amount of money as other online stores. They just positioned their pricing differently. They make their pricing back-loaded instead of front-loaded. They shave off a lot of the price upfront, only to get it back when you checkout.

These websites are set up to exploit people's predictable psychology once they get lowballed. Once you emotionally buy into the prospect of buying that product for a certain price, it's hard to let go.

For some people, this is a matter of pride. In their minds, they've already committed. They have basically given up looking for that exact same product from other places.

For other people, they are just simply lazy. They think that this deal already answered their questions. They're tired of looking for a bigger and better deal.

Whatever the individual reason, it's very hard for them to let go of the deal. That's how these comparison websites with misleading pricing make a lot of money. That is their business plan. It's all about milking the lowball manipulation strategy for all its worth.

The fact that these websites rake in a tremendous amount of money day after day is a testament to the effectiveness of this technique.

Mechanics of the Lowball Technique

The first step is to get the other person to sign on to the deal. How do you do this? Well, first of all, you have to give them the precise products and services that they're looking for.

There has to be a direct fit. They have to be interested in the first place.

These are not impulse buyers. These are not people who are normally not interested. These are people who are already interested in what you have to offer.

The next step is the lowball offer. It has to be clear that this product is normally priced this much. If you are promoting to the right people, they would already know this. They would know the average price of the item and would see that the price that you're offering is indeed a bargain.

It's very important to make sure that the price is low enough, yet believable. This is the key.

If you're going to lure somebody in with a lowball manipulation technique, you cannot say that you are giving somebody a MacBook Air for $1. That's an obvious giveaway. In fact, you can be a blind person and see that a mile away.

It has to look believable. So let's say the product or service you're offering generally sells for $1,000, offering it for $690, even $750, is realistically low.

You can make a stronger point if you do price comparisons. You basically take snapshots or some sort of report summary of the pricing offered by other places.

The next step is to get the person to sign on to the deal. If they've done their homework, they know that this is a good deal. So they come in and they're ready to commit.

It's important, for legal purposes, not to make a formal offer. This cannot be a formal offer. Basically, you are just offering a quotation and then they have to go to a next step for the condition.

This is crucial. Because if you do this wrong, you may be on the hook for the original low price.

You have to be clear on the terms and conditions of your website or in the terms and conditions of your sales materials or initial sales contact that this is just a preliminary offer. Once they're in, in a relatively short period of time, follow up with the condition. Basically, you're saying, "Yes, this is the price, but that does not include taxes, shipping and handling, or processing."

Alternatively, you could say, "This is the package product, but it's missing this other item." And if they do their research, they know that this other item is what really delivers the value for the whole package.

Whatever the case may be, this technique works based on incomplete information. You are in total control of the information going in, and then you drop it on them at the final stage.

What Makes This Technique So Powerful?

This manipulation technique is so potent because it exploits people's need for closure.

Remember, they are looking for a solution. They thought they found the solution in your offer and they are emotionally pumped up. They think that they're getting a good deal and then you drop the bomb and tell them that there's a missing piece. They have to pay extra.

While the conversion rate of this technique is not 100%, it's high up there because there are many things going on. First of all, people feel that, in the big scheme of things, your offer is still good enough even if they factor in taxes.

Also, there's a sense of relief because they feel that you already offered a solution and you are just freeing them from the hassle of looking for a better solution.

Finally, there is a sense of pride and emotional connection. They are already emotionally bound to that offer. They already bought in at some level before.

Whatever the individual reason may be, this lowball technique has a very high conversion rate, but it has to be executed just right.

As I've mentioned above, it cannot look unrealistic that it's easy to dismiss as some sort of scam or gimmick. It also has to be followed up very quickly because you are trying to strike while the iron is hot.

Remember, when a person mentally says, "You've sold me on that initial low offer," they're emotionally hot. They're very persuadable at that point. You cannot let them cool down.

Because once you let some time pass, they may start thinking about other things going on in their lives. Maybe their water heater broke down, maybe their kid's piano teacher needs to get paid – they start thinking about other issues and the emotional urgency of your offer dies down.

Don't let that happen. You have to follow up very quickly.

Chapter 7 : Chameleon Effect : Convince Others About Your Perspective

Imagine for a moment walking through a savanna landscape hundreds of thousands of years ago. You and your tiny band of prehistoric humans are going through your hunting trails. As you cross vast grasslands, you come across another band of hunters. This makes for a very tense moment. You don't quite know what to expect.

However, as you get closer to their group, a lot of the initial tension goes away. How come? You notice that they have the same spears as you. They tend to dress the same way and, most importantly, they share a very similar language. You have a lot in common and you hit it off. They share their campfire fire with you. You share the stuff that you foraged and this otherwise tense meeting ends happily.

Now, what if we made some changes to that situation and you come across people who look very different from you. How would you respond? If your initial response was to simply treat them like people you know, you may have a problem. They may be hostile. There's really no way of knowing; but chances are quite good that if these people were very similar to you, there would be no bloodshed, violence or some sort of misunderstanding.

If your group did not have this built-in preference for familiarity with people who look similar, there are going to be very few of you left. How many times can you take the chance of mixing with strangers only to end up with a few dead band members? It's only a matter of time until your band of hunter foragers die out. Your genes don't make it to the next generation.

Human beings, for the most part, have this built-in preference for familiarity. We tend to like people who look like us, behave like us and talk like us. We feel more comfortable around them and we are more likely to be persuaded when we feel we are dealing with people who are familiar enough.

This is where the chameleon effect comes in. You take advantage of this deep-seated human psychological bias for familiarity. When you are talking to somebody you are trying to persuade, pick up on their body language. Pay attention to the words they use. Look at their mannerisms.

There are three general types of people when it comes to body language communication.

First, there are **visual people**. They tend to look better. They tend to have a better appearance because they are visual people. They pay close attention to what they can see so looks have a high premium with them. They like to look good, look clean and proper.

They also expect people to look at them in the eye when they're talking.

Finally, when you're communicating with visual people, talk about how you can "see where they're coming from." Tell them that you can visualize their idea. They think in visual terms. That's how they make sense of the world.

Visual people make up around 75% of the population. The **other 20% are people who are hearers**.

They are auditory by nature. They become uncomfortable if you look at them in the eye for too long. They tend to look sideways. They tend to listen before they talk. They tend to be on the quiet side.

They also would prefer to handle something that creates a noise. Maybe they would tap their fingers on the table or they would keep clicking on a pan. That's how they tune in and remain engaged. They are also very analytical by nature. They talk less and think more.

Finally, there are touchy, feely people. These are tactile individuals. They make sense of the world based on their sense of touch and emotion. These individuals are more likely to embrace and hug the first time they meet you. They say smile a lot and communicate in terms of their feelings and emotions.

When dealing with auditory people, make sure you avoid looking at them in the eye for too long. Get eye contact then quickly look to the side or look up to avoid further eye contact. If you keep looking at them in the eyes, it's going to make them feel uncomfortable.

Also, when you are making your point or replying, use phrases like "I hear you" or "this sounds like..." They navigate the world based on their sense of hearing.

They also tend to be slower in response because they tend to think things through. They think and process before they talk.

When dealing with tactile people, phrase your statements in terms of "I feel that..." or "I empathize with..." Let your emotions shine through. Be more transparent with what you're feeling and try to communicate warmth, connection and bonding.

The chameleon effect is all about mirroring the communication style and personal orientation of the person in front of you. When you do so, you start looking more familiar to them. You're less of a threat. They are more likely to open up. More importantly, they are more likely to trust you. By going to where they are and mirroring their communication style, you become more persuasive.

There is a limit to this however. You cannot be obvious about it. When somebody is an obvious auditory person, you cannot all of a sudden turn into this turn into a stereotypical auditory person where you stop looking people in the eye and start clicking on a pen. It doesn't work that way.

A little bit goes a long way when it comes to mirroring. You cannot just automatically transform into the mirror persona of the person you're communicating with. That's too obvious. At the very least, they would suspect you're trying to pull something. Something's not right. Instead of establishing rapport and building mutual comfort, they become very suspicious.

Sometimes this can blow up in your face. If, for example, you're dealing with a tactile person and you come off as mocking them or somehow making fun of their emotional displays, you would get the opposite of what you're looking for.

You're looking to be understood. You're looking for agreement. Don't be surprised if you are perceived as some sort of troll that you get pushed back or even flat-out opposition.

The Secret to Effective Mimicry: Make it Look Non-conscious

The more automatic your mimicking behavior looks, the more likely you'll get the outcome you're shooting for.

Based on a study out of New York University published in 1999, researchers saw that there was a greater empathy between people when study participants mimicked study subjects.

Study participants were asked to if they liked the person in photographs that they were reviewing. When the study participant looked at a photograph that mimicked the participant's posture, mannerism and body movements, they tended to like the person in the photo.

A control group was set up where the pictures of the people were random. It turns out that, with everything else being equal, people have a built-in bias for others who are similar enough to them.

Chemeleon effect can help you build a quick rapport with other people; they will start to connect better with you and as a result, you can convince them to move towards the actions that you wanted them to do.

Chapter 8 : How Decoy Effect Makes Your Preferred Option Stand Out

When people are made to choose between two options, it's very easy for them to go with their built-in preference. The problem is if you're trying to persuade them to take your option, this might not be all that good for you. It may turn out that the option you're trying to sell to your audience is an inferior choice.

How do you make your product stand out when it has a serious deficit? Maybe it's missing a feature. Perhaps it underperforms in some key metric. Maybe it costs more.

One way to make your option look really good to your audience is to use the decoy effect. By default, your product, service, cause or advocacy may, on its face, look inferior to an obviously superior option.

These shortcomings are only obvious if there are only two choices. If given a choice between what you're promoting and another option, chances are your prospects would choose the other option most of the time.

Introduce a third option that makes your option look reasonable and play up its strong point. For example, if you are trying to convince people to buy a product that is expensive, has a moderate speed and delivers average quality, you should line it up with a product that is extremely expensive, very fast and produces high quality.

The other option is a product that produces high quality but is very slow and is moderately priced. You have to line up the choices based on the strength of your product. In this case, your strength is your speed, your middle of the road.

So you create a brochure or a webpage that plays up the speed of the service. When people look through the charts and read the reviews and, most importantly, when you play up the combination of speed and moderate pricing, chances are your product would sell better.

This is the decoy effect. It's all about comparison. Remember people determine value by asking a very important question: Compared to what? That's how intelligent people make decisions. You can use this against them and manipulate this logic by playing up your strong suit.

If have a slow and expensive product, you're not going to make a big deal out of those points. You're not going to score too many points with those. You find something else that your product dominates in.

The good news is if you do your research, there is at least one area you are going to dominate in. Put that front and center and then line up all the competing products based on your dominant position.

In other words, fight on a battlefield that you dominate. You can't compete on price. You may not be able to compete on equality durability, the whole nine yards. However, if you can find one or a couple of areas where you can dominate, play those up.

Also, it helps to cherry-pick the competition. Look for competitors that are well known but are expensive, take too long to deliver or has serious durability issues. As much as you can, look for otherwise high-quality or well-known products that are really weak in the areas your product dominates in.

In a 1981 Duke University study, researchers split up groups of study participants and asked them which restaurant they would choose. In the first group, only two options were presented. Participants had a choice between a five-star restaurant, which was located twenty-five minutes away and three-star restaurant that was located five minutes away. In this two-option group, everybody was asked to choose based on their personal preferences.

Another group was given three options. In addition to five-star and three-star restaurant, a four-star restaurant was added to the mix but this one was located thirty-five minutes away. It turns out that in the second group, people chose the five-star restaurant. It highlighted the quality of the restaurant and downplayed the drive.

The key dilemma here is to choose between the quality of the food and convenience. When presented a "decoy" that played up the five-star rating of the restaurant and made its distance seem reasonable, most people chose that option.

The decoy effect really all boils down to playing to your strengths. Whatever proposition you may have, there will always be an area where your proposition will dominate. Play that up.

Whatever you're offering might not be the cheapest, the highest quality or the fastest. Regardless, find an area where you can dominate and then line up your competition to highlight your area of dominance. That's how you increase sales conversions.

Believe it or not, using the decoy technique, you can manipulate people in such a way that you can turn your lemons into lemonade.

Chapter 9 : Use the "Even a Penny will Help" to Maximize Extraction

One of the biggest hurdles to getting people to separate with their hard-earned money is the thinking that if people give to some nonprofit or charitable organization, that their small donation really won't go that far.

Basically, they're saying to themselves "My help is not going to make much of a difference. Why even try?" While a lot of people who think this have noble motives, it's very easy to see how this can be used as an excuse to not give.

One of the most effective ways to overcome this is to say an almost magical phrase. "Even a penny will help" or "every penny counts."

When you say this to people you are trying to get donations from, their inhibitions go away. Remember they're carrying around that question. They're unsure whether their small donation is going to make much of a difference.

Well, by saying that statement or a variation of it, you answer that question directly. Yes, your penny will make a difference. Yes, no donation is too small. Yes, everybody can help.

Please note that this technique only increases the likelihood that people will give. It does not increase the amount of their donation. Keep that in mind. This is a volume strategy.

Chapter 10 : "It is Your Choice" Technique– Let Them Feel Hero

One of the most powerful ways to manipulate people is to manipulate them without looking like a manipulator. This is harder than you think. However, it is a worthy goal.

You have to understand that people are prideful. We would like to imagine that the decisions that we come up with are entirely are our own. They are not products of manipulation. We would like to think that we were not the victims of slick salesmanship.

Accordingly, one of the most basic rules of salesmanship, persuasion and, yes, manipulation is to make it look like the choice was made freely by the other party. That's right. The person that you're trying to convince or manipulate must be made to feel that he or she made the choice. You have to make it seem like they came up with the idea. This happens quite a bit because when people feel that they are their own agent, that they are the captain of the ship of their personal destiny, they feel good about themselves. Everybody has this.

When you use the "it's your choice" strategy, you tap into this. This is a strong psychological need that all people from all over the world, from different cultures, different backgrounds, different times, and different religions share. We all would like to believe that we have a choice. We would all like to believe that we call the shots, at least when it comes to our personal lives.

When you use this technique, you put the ball in their court. What this does is you manipulate their need to be validated based on their ability to make decisions.

I want you to think about this. Since the initiative came from you, is it really their choice? Is it really their idea?

When you say the phrase "it's your choice" or "you are free to choose," you are triggering this mechanism. The reality is you put the offer to them. You made the initiative. You took the first step. You reached out.

However, the key here is to not let them see that. You definitely don't want to give them the impression that it is you calling the shots or pulling the strings. Choose whatever metaphor you want.

The bottom line is to close that sale. At the end of the day, it doesn't really matter how much credit you get. What's important is you close the deal. Get them to sign on the dotted line. "Always be closing," to borrow a very famous phrase from the classic film Glengarry Glen Ross.

You have to use the phrase "It's your choice" and "you are free to choose" the right way. You can't just say them in passing. You have to make your case and then look the person in the eye depending on their communication style.

This is crucial. If a person is visual by nature, this is fine; but if the person is auditory, meaning they don't like eye contact; they tend to look to the side and down, and they either move their hands or click something that they can hear or they tap their fingers on the table, you might want to quick eye contact, look to the side and the bottom and then say it. Say the offer and then say the phrase "it's your choice."

Just how effective is this technique? In a study published in 2000 out of the University of Bordeaux, researchers found that if they demanded money and followed it up with "but you are free to accept or to refuse," the prospects actually complied at a higher rate than the control group.

What's interesting about this study involving charitable donations is this technique not only increases the likelihood that people will donate money; it also boosts the amount donated. Very fascinating results because it's very different from the "even a penny will help" approach. The latter approach increases the rate of compliance but doesn't really increase the amount of money raised.

When you say people are free to choose accepting or refusing, they not only tend to comply more, they tend to give more.

Conclusion

The art of manipulation is exactly that. It's an art. While there is a tremendous amount of science that goes behind manipulation as you can tell from the citations in this book, at the end of the day, it's an art. How come?

Well, when you try to manipulate people in different circumstances, situations change. You're not always dealing with the same type of person. You're not always dealing with optimal conditions.

The great thing about experiments is that there are variables that can be controlled. Not so with real life. Accordingly, while it is tempting to say that persuasion can be boiled down to some sort of hard science, you really can't be so sure. You still have to play it by ear.

At the very least, look at the ten techniques that I have shared with you in this book as a tool kit. Size up the person that you are dealing with. Try to figure out what they're about, what they're looking for, the kind of questions that they're asking and the problems that they're trying to solve. You then line that up with the objective you want to see happen.

Whether you're trying to get people to vote for a candidate, buy one product over another or subscribe to a service or go home with you at night, you have to personalize manipulation. You cannot use some sort of one-size-fits-all, magic-bullet approach. That's not going to work.

Remember each and every person you will meet is an individual. Everybody's different. Everybody looks at the world with a different pair of eyes. We all have different experiences. All these small differences add up.

This is why you have to be very careful in sizing up people and making educated guesses in your head as to which tools from your kit you're going to use. This book prepares you for manipulation because let's get one thing clear, if you want to achieve any kind of success in this world, you have to be persuasive. You have to make your case.

Unfortunately, most of the time, your situation and prospects will be far from ideal. This is why you need to be quick on your feet and master the art of reading your situation so you can tackle it with your best tool.

I wish you nothing but success!

DISCLAIMER

commands. The reader is responsible for his or her own actions.

The author makes no representations or warranties with respect to the accuracy or completeness of the contents of this work and specifically disclaims all warranties, including without limitation warranties of fitness for a particular purpose. No warranty may be created or extended by sales or promotional materials. The advice and recipes contained herein may not be suitable for everyone. This work is sold with the understanding that the author is not engaged in rendering medical, legal or other professional advice or services. If professional assistance is required, the services of a competent professional person should be sought. The author shall not be liable for damages arising here from. The fact that an individual, organization of website is referred to in this work as a citation and/or potential source of further information does not mean that the author endorses the information the individual, organization to website may provide or recommendations they/it may make. Further, readers should be aware that Internet websites listed in this work might have

changed or disappeared between when this work was written and when it is read.

Adherence to all applicable laws and regulations, including international, federal, state, and local governing professional licensing, business practices, advertising, and all other aspects of doing business in any jurisdiction in the world is the sole responsibility of the purchaser or reader.

Printed in Great
Britain
by Amazon

31471437R00051